Delphi Series
Vol VIII

featuring

Carly Sachs
Lois Marie Harrod
Charlotte Mandel

Published by Blue Lyra Press

Copyright © 2020 BLUE LYRA PRESS
All rights reserved.

ISBN-: 978-1-7338909-8-4

Blue Lyra Review, a journal of diverse voices, is a division of *Blue Lyra Press*, and it is currently closed to new submissions.

Blue Lyra Press publishes several times a year and accepts poetry and flash fiction chapbook submissions under 25 pages during two months throughout each year: January and July only. Send directly to the email below.

Writings or images published on the *Blue Lyra Review* website or in print are copyrighted by the creators. Explicit permission must be obtained from the copyright holder for use of any such material. E-mail bluelyrareview@gmail.com to obtain contact information for those writers and artists.

Blue Lyra Review & *Blue Lyra Press* are independent and rely solely on the generosity of donations so **please** support the arts: (**www.bluelyrareview.com/donations/**).

SUBMISSIONS: direct to email with bio, acknowledgments, and table of contents

FACEBOOK: www.facebook.com/BlueLyraPress

TWITTER: twitter.com/MESilverman_BLP

PURCHASE: bluelyrapress.com/

CORRESPONDENCE: bluelyrareview@gmail.com

Front Cover: Alicia Armstrong's *Emergence (23)*

Front Cover Design: Claire Zoghb

Note to Readers

It is my delight to introduce you to the third book in the Delphi Series in a long time. This why BLP switched the numbering of the books to roman numerals. After a long absence and the closing of our sister journal, Blue Lyra Review, we are proud to introduce three amazing chapbooks. I hope you enjoy it as much as I do! This single bound book consists of three separate chapbooks by three separate poets bound in one single volume. Why would anyone do this? Good question! I think you, the reader, picked this book up because you are interested in one of the poets within these bound pages. In doing so, you are now exposed to two other poets. Maybe you heard of them before you picked this book up; maybe you didn't. But, it's like getting 3 books for the price of 1!

The series opens with *Descendants of Eve* by Carly Sachs and immediately Marcela Sulak said of Sachs that she "examines the varieties of love—parental, romantic, spiritual, ecological, generational—through the lens of her own conception and practice of Judaism; or maybe she examines Judaism through the varieties of love." I agree. As she clarifies in the opening poem, "I will sing. / Out of this. I am calling. / The body is a music." And truly this is a musical manuscript of wondrous poems. Some of my favorite poems set Adam and Eve in a contemporary scene. "Eve in the Meanwhile," for instance, is about the endings of first love and after, Eve buys a bag of apples on sale. "It was all / I could muster, / seeds and core. / It left me wanting." And I have no doubt that reading here will leave you wanting more as well, more of Sachs's eloquent sentiment.

The next chapbook is equally marvelous. Doty said Harrod's collection is simply but perfectly called Woman. Harrod's work is filled with "natural music, sharp observations and sly wit [that] brings a quirky authenticity to her tales of women often silenced, missing parts, or completely disassembled." My favorite is the Marlene Mae series that nears the end of the chapbook. But even from the beginning, the chapbook's use of a universal Woman grabs the reader's attention from the beginning with "Woman licks her way into the earth, / no stranger / to her own body, / hair tasting of turnip, / lungs bleating beet." The poems within move from magical realism like in "The Woman Who Lost her Heart" where the Woman "panicked and searched the usual places—windowsill, magazines, the top of the dresser" to narrative persona poems like in the Marlene Mae poems and in "Grandmother." All together, these are remarkable poems that walk the perfect tightrope between beautiful simplicity and poetic wonder.

And finally, the chapbook that ends this series is Mandel's *Light's Music*. Mary Frances Wagner said this book "focuses on both beginnings and ends. In her grandchildren and great grandchildren, she celebrates new life and her legacy going forward, her Jewish heritage honored and preserved—all from a voice reconciling and making close getaways from the inevitable as she prepares for the day "shadows come forth" and she can "dissolve" and rise "to rose-red smoke." This chapbook is a strong distillation of precision in poetry and hope for us all." This can be seen throughout the chapbook. In my favorite poem, "Beach Comber", Mandel reveals the gifts of the sea, both the natural and the unnatural, as the poet looks for shells, "clues to their births and passings." Mandel writes "Fingers grainy with sand / scoop up sun-baked gifts of past tides, / layer white clam shells / one upon the next larger / and seek unbroken / lush purple spirals of moon snail." This is, without a single doubt, "script / that comes forth / in light."

Table of Contents

Descendants of Eve by Carly Sachs   1

Woman by Lois Marie Harrod   29

Light's Music by Charlotte Mandel   67

Critical Praise   102

More from BLP   104

Descendants of Eve

by

Carly Sachs

for Ruthie

Table of Contents

acknowledgments	4
Clarification	5
Adam and Eve on the Upper East Side	6
Adam and Eve in Sunset Park	7
Eve Contemplates Adam and Shame	8
Eve Returns	9
Eve in the Meanwhile	10
Eve, Alone	12
Notes on Leaving	13
Skateboarding Lesson	14
Talmud Study	15
Postcard from Eve	16
Marriage Ceremony, Kibbutz Nir Am, 1948	17
Aubade	18
The Rabbi's Wife	19
Fasting	20
Erev Erev Yom Kippur	21
Mourner's Kaddish, a variation	22
Poem After Mussar	23
Poem for the Man Who Called Me a JewBu	25
Because	26
Biography	28

Acknowledgements

Some of the poems in this chapbook first appeared in the following books and journals:

"Mourner's Kaddish, a variation." Regrets Only. Little Pear Press, 2006.

Poem for the Man Who Called Me a JewBu," Jewish Journal. Los Angeles, CA: March 8-14, 2013.

"Talmud Study," Jewish Journal. Los Angeles, CA: March 29-April 4, 2013.

"Adam and Eve on the Upper East Side" Ducts (Winter 2009).

"Because," Presentense (Spring 2008).

"Postcard from Eve," and "Clarification," Nextbook (April 2008).

"Marriage Ceremony, Kibbutz Nir Am, 1948," No Tell Motel (2005).

CLARIFICATION

The voice is both dagger and feather,
a black curtain, night opens the show.
I mean our hands catch fire. I mean erev.
I mean I was wrong when I said

I always wanted to be a folk singer.
Pass me a note, pass me the salt,

pass me your tears. Ask the Rebbe.
I mean you should seriously rock out.

I mean dehydration. I always wanted
to learn how to French braid, to French

kiss. It was the year before that.
I always wanted your money, or

was it a pony? I always wanted a bouquet
of nothing. I will answer. I will sing.

Out of this. I am calling you.
The body is a music.

The body is an egg.
What is being born?

Wrap your arms around him
and sway. I mean something Hassidic.

I mean Aramaic. I mean saxophone.
I mean bodies. I mean quiet. I mean electric.

ADAM AND EVE ON THE UPPER EAST SIDE

You and I tangled threads of who we were
    and who we are. The ease
of our arms. Our bodies
    snaking around each other.
In a few days, you will buy avocados
    and tomatoes for me.
I will touch the books on your shelves
    and decide you are both
who I thought you were and
    not at all the man
I have loved before love became
    something else besides want.
Here is our stove, our mantle with pictures,
    the radiator, my naked breasts
in the living room. You will pick me up
    and carry me to the bed. It is
as it was. It will never be as it was.

ADAM AND EVE IN SUNSET PARK

It should have been perfect, our own
    little Eden. The backyard
in Brooklyn, the brownstone we wanted,
    the boredom
of beauty, grapevines snaking up
    the back of the house,
me making Eggs Benedict, the beauty
    of boredom
on Sunday mornings. The sun tic-tac-
    toeing our checkered floor,
the game going on before us.
    Who's X's and who's O's,
the two of us facing each other
    at the table.

EVE CONTEMPLATES ADAM AND SHAME

Your name means man
>though your arms
could be anyone's. The difference
>between apples
and figs. The pull
>of your ribs,
brushstroke of desire
>or punishment, the memory
of my hand reaching up.
>What is it I wanted
in that moment, or even now,
>how much of it
distinguishable from any other
>man, any other
woman.

EVE RETURNS

How then do we come back to each other:
changed, unchanged,
a lifetime or nothing between us?
Is your hand only your hand
or everything else you've touched?
How then can I love you,
or because we have unraveled
can I now love you?
What purpose did it all serve—
the fruit, the snake
that longing for perfection?
What do any of us know of
some other plan, the things
we're destined for, a g-d above
playing the strings.
Call the heart seed
or beast, blood vessels and
veins, roots or ropes.
We come to each other with our bruised and our blame,
our hopes.

EVE IN THE MEANWHILE

They say you never forget
your first.

There was night
and then there was morning.

It was supposed to be that simple,
but whose image were we?

What were we thinking,
carving our initials

into that tree. True love,
forever, we named what we had made:

heart, sex. We drew birds,
wrote it all down,

not knowing the erasure
of permanence.

They say things will change,
they will be subtle at first,

you uncoiling,
but husband, your swagger!

If that was love, I'd rather---
It will be slight, there was night,

it was done, there was morning.
You were gone.

I plucked the apple,
bought a bag full of them on sale

at the grocery. It was all
I could muster,

seeds and core.
It left me wanting

wanting
more.

EVE, ALONE

This half-life
    the with of without
my pair of arms, legs, these breasts
    will have to be enough.
Husband, the memory of you
    snaking around my neck,
between my legs. The shadows arcing
    across the room, the out
then in. The pull of memory---
    how I came out of you,
how I entered you.
    The consecration, then
the sin. Now you with your ashes,
    me with my whiskey.
Is it love or loving you,
    my love, is it true
we have come back
    to be broken.

NOTES ON LEAVING

You come to a well,
there was a choice.

Something was burning.
You felt something.

The text is ambiguous.
There was a vow.

The shepherds were unruly.
Her arm was eight feet long.

She was in the palace.
She was not in the palace.

You write it on a tablet.
Everyone talks about the Cushite woman.

You write it on a tablet.
How do you hide a baby?

All the babies were in the river.
You put your hope in a basket,

and you say the words.
At some point you kill someone.

All around, frogs, boils.
You escape.

There is one word that means lip, edge, or shore.
You part the sea,

it's obvious, only if
you call it obvious.

SKATEBOARDING LESSON

We are becoming men and women
on this day, as you tell someone else's story---

I have no idea which, but I imagine
your voice and the way

those who love you are looking at you.
I think of what I have lost,

the man you are becoming, all the men
I will never know.

My skateboard was pink and came from
Hills Department store.

At your age, I skinned my knees and
gave up.

Even on my friend's Sega, I crashed and burned
at Skate or Die!

But Jason, the board is your breath,
now your heart.

No, your sister, your parents.
It is the sun setting over Jerusalem.

It is a story, it is a book,
it's your entire life.

TALMUD STUDY

How do you measure anything---
count your deaths, who loves you, who loves you not.
Today you are the ox, tomorrow the victim
of the gorging ox.

You build a house, you are holy,
but your walls are shaky.
Inside there is wine to be drunk.
Outside there is a plague.
You are on the wrong page.

Someone is coming to town on a donkey.
He will insult your intelligence
then ask for forgiveness.
Everything is a ratio, parts of the whole.

You watch the ants as they crawl across your plate.
You snuff out every third one with your pinky finger.
Years later they will say, blood, frogs, boils,
but what are they remembering?
Your house is falling---
who is the protagonist and what is it he wants?

POSTCARD FROM EVE

You wake up in Dresden
where shadows have shadows.

A sentence atrophied,
you will order tea

after every meal, the leaves
and spices like the t-shirts

and underwear in your duffel.
You've been steeping in the rain,

in the streets where you speak
to no one.

You will sigh, you had a lover,
once, who carved his name

into your back. A knife
or a tongue, does it matter?

Inside you, someone else's weather.
The taste of snow

in your teeth and no one
to warm you.

MARRIAGE CEREMONY, KIBBUTZ NIR AM, 1948

August
sun

ignites
this

country
of cloth

burning
white

the same
light

trapped
beneath

their skin
there is

more than
one

vow
today

their chuppah
held

up
by four

slender
rifles

AUBADE

A shawl, a tear, a tear, after her, the old women bring Rugelach sprinkled with sugar, your mother will not let anyone remove the sliced tomatoes from the kitchen counter though everyone else wants them in the refrigerator. Your father will return with scotch, a bottle of red, of white It is the last day of the month Earlier while our arms bend as we fill the grave I try to figure out what this sounds like, rain, grief, mine not mine, nothing comes, not shade, not wind, not time, not words. We lower her down, not shade, not wind, not gone. The next morning I will wake hours past dawn.

THE RABBI'S WIFE

There is a rumor that women
who committed adultery in ancient Babylonia
drowned themselves in the mikveh.
Blue bodies rising to Adonai
with hair wild, unbraided.
They looked like mermaids,
mouths in infinite O's.

It was the duty of the rabbi's wife
to collect and prepare the bodies for burial.
In the room next to her husband's study,
she'd work for hours pressing pomegranate seeds
into abandoned flesh.

When she told the husbands the news,
it was always an accident—
the stairs were slippery,
she had a weak heart,
or if the husband was a scholar,
she would send the rabbi to deliver the message.

She always wore gloves,
hair immaculately tucked into her shaytl
when she left the home.

The next morning the water in the mikveh
would be thick as roses,
smell like fruit, rotting.

FASTING

It is
more

than this
hunger

the fish
caught

between what
was and

what is
life

this
thin branch

of beach
during summer's

final
breaths

where
three fishermen

knee deep
in the sound

will not hear
the quiet

death
they make

EREV, EREV YOM KIPPUR

I'm writing this poem on my hand because I want you to know precisely the way everything was. I'm taking notes so you will know the sidewalk looked like cracked marbles, not snow, that the steps to the apartment where Frank O'Hara used to live were covered with rubber bands and old newspapers, not plastic bags, and dog hair. I don't want to give you another sentimental poem so when I tell you that Matt whispered great enchiladas as we passed a Mexican restaurant I want you to expect nothing profound, just a good, cheap meal. When I say it was cold and it was the perfect night for a cigarette, please note that I wasn't wearing a jacket and I don't smoke. I didn't write down the color of the door, but I think it was either jade or olive, and I lifted the mail slot, that's how I knew about the newspapers and rubber bands and ten steps. I counted twice. I tried to picture Frank coming home drunk, bringing a man back to his place, or carrying grocery bags, but I was hungry so I started thinking about the enchiladas again and wondering if I had time to get one before my flight home and I kept thinking this would be a great story for my friends back in Kent, especially Alice because she believes in karma and Frank and I both have ten letters in our names, first and last combined. Here, I feel like I need to mention that it is two days before Yom Kippur and there are ten days between Rosh Hashanah and Yom Kippur where you're supposed to apologize for any misfortunes you may have inflicted on someone else, so if I've left out some details, it's only because I've been quite introspective lately and I guess now is a good time to tell you I'm ambidextrous and quite good at shorthand so you can stop wondering how this entire poem can fit on two hands and if ten fingers, ten days, ten letters, and ten steps need to make any sense.

MOURNER'S KADDISH, A VARIATION

it's not the death we mourn
because it's the death we carry
knowing only that part of the life we lose
is our own

it is a collapsing of the soul like that of a star
and we fear we may forget

so we breathe life back
into scented scarves, vacant mirrors

carry our dead
in embroidered tablecloths,
costume jewelry,
our own names.

POEM AFTER MUSSAR

I lay my body
belly down on the grass.
From here, each little sword,
each little stem,
tiny green stalks of spine waving,
Hello!

This takes me back to seventh grade,
when I calligraphed, the grass must bend,
when the wind blows across it.
I don't remember if it was that line
or that it was attributed to someone
named Confucius.

Did I like that he went by one name,
like Madonna or Prince?
Or that there was the wisdom
coming from confusion, or at least someone
whose name made me think of that.

I am, chirp late afternoon crickets,
the ones that hover and buzz and
go about their business in flight.
How many planes overhead unseen,
And how many faces in windows
aware of motion below?

At temple today, Carol told a story,
How when she worked as a flight attendant
for Delta, they counted passengers,
but when she worked for Alaskan Airlines,
they counted how many souls
were on board.

Below, as a child, I would wave,
Even though I knew they couldn't
see me. My I am-ness,
the buzz of my own motion.

A lone ant crawls across my notebook
on legs smaller than an eyelash.

POEM FOR THE MAN WHO CALLED ME A JEWBU

This is the story of my people:
When Rachel dies bearing a child
whom she names, child of my suffering,
Jacob calls him Benjamin, child of my right hand.

I'm reminded of the man who comes to the bar
who noticed the Star of David around my neck,
my mala beads wound round my left hand
and said are you a JewBu?

I said I'm a Jew who practices yoga,
the star close to my heart, who I am,
the beads on my arm, what I do.
What is the difference between love and action?

Outside the Krishna temple there is a bell
on the right side, you're supposed to ring it
when you enter, which is what Ragunath, my yoga teacher
tells me and so I do.

It was a Saturday morning and I was not in temple.
Upstairs the sunlight on my purple mat.
I did not say the bell reminded me of the mezuzah,
which my people affix to the doorposts of their houses,

how we kiss it when entering and leaving.
What is the difference between alike and different?
Where Rachel died, Jacob put a pillar
to explain something unexplainable.

BECAUSE

Because these words existed before
they could fill our mouths

Because our parents said them
and our grandparents and great-

grandparents because they echo
until they shed their meaning

becoming syllables of ember,
lit matches winging

to Yahrzeit candles.
Because Warsaw,

Because we slam doors
on those we love

Because the floor boards creak
as we walk room to room

because someone knows where we are,
where we belong. Because months,

because fire, because sweets, because
crumbs, because holes, because seeds,

because we are born
to repeat and they are born

to tune out
until it is the voice

of memory and her hands
stitching a loop:

because I love you, because
I said so, because

I love you, I love
you, I love you

Author's Bio

Carly Sachs is the author of *the steam sequence* and the editor of the anthology *the why and later*, a collection of poems about rape and assault. Her poems and stories have been included in The Best American Poetry Series and read on NPR's Selected Shorts. She writes, teaches yoga, and lives in Lexington, Kentucky where she serves as the co-director for PJ Library.

Woman

by

Lois Marie Harrod

For Katherine and Sophia

Table of Contents

acknowledgements	32
Woman	33
Her Body	34
Reclining Woman with Green Stockings	35
Large Reclining Nude	37
The Woman Who Lost Her Heart	38
The Woman Who Put Herself Back Together	40
The Woman Who Found Things	42
The Woman without a Heart	44
The Other Woman	45
The Woman Who Never Said a Word	47
The Motorcyclist's Woman Browses All Love Poems	48
The Widow Sees His Face as a Strange Flower	49
The Widow Laments Another Autumn	50
Icarus's Mother Talks to Her Son	51
Marlene Mae Warns of Travel to Her Former Marriage	53
Marlene Mae Talks about Denial	54
Marlene Mae's Mother Turns Seventy-Six and Her Physician Asks if She Is Still Sexually Active	55
Marlene Mae Paints Her Mother's Nails	57
Grandmother	58
The True Believer Works in the Vineyard	60
Woman Finds Her Face	62
The Widow's Self-Portrait in Quicksand	63
Shelf-Portrait	64
Biography	65

Acknowledgments

Bellingham Review: Marlene Mae Talks about Denial, Marlene Mae's Mother Turns Seventy-Six and Her Physician Asks if She Is Still Sexually Active
Casa de Cinco Hermanas: The Woman Who Lost Her Heart
Cimarron Review: Grandmother
Ekphrasis: Reclining Woman with Green Stockings
Fourth River: The True Believer Works in the Vineyard
The Mid-America Poetry Review: Large Reclining Nude
The Mom Egg: Marlene Mae Paints Her Mother's Nails
Number One: Marlene Mae Warns of Travel to Her Former Marriage
Pink Panther Magazine: Her Body, Woman
Pittsburgh Poetry Review: The Woman without a Heart
River Styx: Woman Finds Her Face
Sliver of Stone: The Woman Who Put Herself Back Together
Sycamore: Shelf-Portrait
Schuylkill Valley Journal: The Widow Sees His Face as a Strange Flower
U. S. 1: The Woman Who Found Things
Weatherings (Future Cycle Press): The Widow Laments Another Autumn
Weber: The Contemporary West: Icarus's Mother Talks to Her Son

WOMAN

licks her way into the earth,
no stranger
to her own body,
hair tasting of turnip,
lungs bleating beet,
and heart, her heart,
the hibernating bear.
How long will she sleep,
slow her breath,
root those dreams,
those double-helix ladders
to the stars?
Belly, nest and bladder
moss and mushroom,
come eat.
Simple and concentric,
world wrapped in world
wrapping world,
the small animal
forming inside her, turning.
Now she feels it
fleet down
her mole ways,
rest in her mouse crib,
and here within,
a cot unto itself,
hold and unfold
within without,
cave closed in cave,
bubble swaddled in bubble,
babble swathed in babble,
the weaker vessel Plato
could not shadow
or shut down.

HER BODY

Now the canyon face, strata
to strata, the deep divide: ribs

rising and falling within the ancient loom,
dry weave hefting desert shanks,

gulch at window, rift and gorge.
What of earth is not my body?

Curtains coil tornadoes like water
falling, years twist the double helix.

Let the inner gorge be wet, the upland talus
smooth to the inside of clam,

the glossy silt within a woman's body,
the milk that sleeks us into being.

Now drift and eminence, mount
upland canyon, gorge, basin, dell—

we could die like this
in swales and troughs,

the drapes of morning drawing in
the drapes of night drawing out.

RECLINING WOMAN WITH GREEN STOCKINGS

      after Egon Schiele

There is nothing
in the world but my body

reclining on a sheet
of blank paper, my body

and its mock array
green stockings cut mid thigh

the leggy street stains
the ivory slip

just enough to remind me
I exist.

When I dress
I garb the universe

the slightest scarf
a galaxy

and then I disappear
ladder up the heel

and those others beyond me
objects before light.

What of you
when you are gone?

I pull my knee to my chest
a continent

but not big enough to be

the bed I'm sleeping in-

no red wallpaper, please
no funereal chrysanthemums

just sex and death
gouache and black crayon.

LARGE RECLINING NUDE

after Matisse's *Pink Nude*

I said to him I said
why did you make me so big
and why did you make
the white bedspread
look like a black and white
tiled floor, do you want
people to think I let you take
me in the kitchen, you know
there is no way I could fit
between the refrigerator
and the sink, there
just isn't enough room there
to jam me, the size of that body,
and he said,
sometimes you seem
that big to me.

THE WOMAN WHO LOST HER HEART

At first she didn't realize it was missing, her heart, and then she panicked, searched the usual places—windowsill, magazines, the top of the dresser with her rings. Maybe she had wrapped it up with the linen when she changed the bed or maybe it had fallen out of her chest when she had opened the door to grab the mail.

She began again methodically, retracing her steps through her rooms—the closet where she tossed her shoes and the bathtub where she found her hair. Where was it? She didn't know anyone who could steal her heart away.

Her friends told her not to worry, go on with life, they said. A cousin mentioned that her spleen had been gone for a year before her daughter found it in the library lost-and-found. An old schoolmate discovered her spine in the glove compartment after her husband had that terrible crash on Route 95. Don't worry, said her therapist, hearts have a way of coming back. But the woman's chest felt empty as it had when her diamond had come loose in the dishwater and drifted down the drain. One night she woke suddenly, like a woman electro-shocked back to life. For a moment her heart seemed to have returned, to be trembling inside her, but when she felt her pulse, nothing . . . nothing there.

THE WOMAN WHO PUT HERSELF BACK TOGETHER

Every morning the same difficulties, first
to find a surface flat enough to work, then

to dump the pieces and face them up. She
began with the corners as she had been taught,

but today, where was the fourth? She'd have
to dig in her purse again. She went on

to the edges but gaps appeared between
the eyebrow and roof of that little white

cottage with its immaculate curtains, the row
of spruce seemed to have mysteriously

thinned, and the center pieces which had once
been crisp and firm had become cardboard

her dog had chewed. Some friends said she was
going about the puzzle all wrong, she should

sort what's left into tabs and blanks, see what
fit where, but this morning she couldn't tell

the innies from the outies. Even her belly
button seemed cryptic. Others advised using

colors to discern the forehead from a firmament,
but she found it increasingly

difficult to filter her hair from the gray fog
that stretched over the valley. The once

smooth swaths of lawn ploughed and furrowed
in unexpected ways, and when she turned

to the picture that had been on the front
of the box, it too looked gnawed and worried.

Her rich friends said she should have had
that first face lift ages ago, and the eco-friends

said that was cheating. You had to play
with the nature you were dealt. It seemed

that there were some sink holes that could
no longer be filled, the pieces had been lost

probably now in China. She thought of her
friend Irene who also appeared to be

having trouble lining up the eyeliner.
The mascara shunted from eyelid to chin.

THE WOMAN WHO FOUND THINGS

Take her with you on a walk and dollar bills leap among the leaves and stainless steel bottle openers twist from the weeds, and then the bottle too, muddy but uncorked, a Malbec from 2010. Her hands seemed magnets that drew what had been discarded, cast off, hidden from another life into her own—a box of firecrackers, a travel cup, briefs tangled in the crown vetch, a red bra. Look what happened here, she'd say, poking a stick into them, carrying them down the road like a flag of discovery—our Mary Leakey of the mundane, Christopher Columbus of the unclean, hats, gloves, socks, watches still ticking, what looked like a wedding ring, tossed she said, no doubt, by a man who was driving by, arguing with his wife about her most recent affair. Take her to a second-hand store and she'd be the one to find the Jimmy Choo boots and the Prabal Gurang dress wadded in a cardboard box and she'd explain how they got there. There was a sort of authority in her stories, as if the objects themselves spoke to her though she didn't claim psychic smarts or archeological evidence of hobbit-like humans on the island of Flores, Indonesia. So we just liked to walk with her and listen to her stories, and no, she had no idea how she did this or why we too couldn't find such stuff. She didn't scare children, who sometimes seemed to have some of her ability, but there were adults among us who found her glittering eye frightening and somehow alien. And no, she couldn't find what we asked her to find, say our glasses or car keys, or that magazine we had just been reading. And no, it was never what we really wanted to find in our own lives, the prodigal son or the daughter who had wandered away and come back with an addiction though sometimes we wondered where her own children had gone.

THE WOMAN WITHOUT A HEART

It was a misconception that the Woman without a
    Heart
had no heart. It was there thudding like everyone
    else's,
just didn't drum faster or not that much faster
when the Man of Her Life entered the room. What
    could
she do? She remembered the sneer on the face of
    her psychologist
when she said, she'd rather read a book. Pleasure
    for pleasure,
reading lasted a lot longer than an orgasm, even a
    novella,
and she was thinking *Remembrance of Things Past*
and *Gone with the Wind*. Eventually, the Woman
    without a Heart
learned she could call herself *asexual* like sex
among bacteria or *semi-sexual* like a truck that had
    lost its trailer
or *gray* or *grey sexual* as if the *a* or *e* was
    interchangeable,
somewhere on the sexual spectrum, no blues or
    greens
or reds or violets, no *tingly fireworks,* no *waves*
    crashing,
earth quaking, cosmic sneeze, nothing that jolted her
    into joy.
Sometimes she asked her partner, what it was he felt,
why did he like sex so much, but she had begun to
    feel
such questions were unkind.

THE OTHER WOMAN

Half a bowl of porridge
and a broken chair

termites and dry rot,
even a bear

feels uncomfortable
when the whatever

comes knocking
and stays to sleep

wanton
and worn out

upstairs–
and just as bad

when the boy
who promised

to love forever
leaves you

with a second child.
Love unfaltering

altered.
Gold and locks–

he'll pay through the nose
that's all he thinks

and you,
my blonde darling,

you wonder
how you will live alone

with ursine
prowling.

THE WOMAN WHO NEVER SAID A WORD

She was the one without eyes
or ears

the one who lost her breasts
first one and then the other

and the one without hands
right or left

to offer her breasts
upon a plate.

She lost
her heart to a sword

and cradled her mouthless head
in her arms

until she misplaced
her feet.

    * * *

Our Leader liked
to rally his troops

with imitations of her
worming her way

through his
jeering mob.

THE MOTOCYCLIST'S WOMAN BROWSES ALL LOVE POEMS

Contemplates her categories—
desire, heartache, loss, romantic
classic, infatuation & crush
unrequited, undelighted
breakups, vexations, last & first—

Tries to refine her search.

He told her, didn't he,
I do not trust a man
who does not love something—
but she is woman, what does she want?

Chocolate or bratwurst
and is this love or is it just longing
for pizza with rye malt
and then a ride
into the Wisconsin Dells?

THE WIDOW SEES HIS FACE
AS A STRANGE FLOWER

Like a bee, now, she must keep busy,
and so she sees his face as a strange flower
and once mounting the hollyhock, she sees too
her other self, one of the Painted Ladies, *Vanessa
      virginiensis*
that ubiquitous butterfly with its two blind eyes on
      each wing,
how could she not have noticed all those years,
food for my larva, and he did provide,
though sometimes grudgingly, yes,
the second child had been hard on him,
and she had turned in, turned aside—
what is the difference between rejection
and depression? anther and stigma.
Certainly nothing that a flower
can comprehend, how often
they did not understand the other,
but now this, how completely he had turned away.
Often she had been something else,
the rabbit to his briar patch, protection, it's true,
but difficult to negotiate, lying down
on a bed of nails, something he seemed
good at, pricks and prickles. Yes, why
hadn't she been more generous,
the pond to the frog, the loam to the worm,
why couldn't she have been what
she had so long thought she was?

THE WIDOW LAMENTS ANOTHER AUTUMN

He planted trees
to make new this world–
as many as our plot
could bear.

For he was that kind
of man, one who
husbanded his acorns
against the sky descending.

Seed against sorrow,
he said, shade to cool
the warming woe.
The little we can do.

But he did not
foresee the fallout
of his un-wiving–
the thousand leaves.

Unsweatered and bare-armed
I rake and rake.
I do not know why
I live so long.

ICARUS'S MOTHER TALKS TO HER SON

I was not given your father's
        engineering mind

and the harpies refuse to bear
        me up.

So I act a life and sometimes live
        it unconsciously

a moment now and now,
        but then

my son, you are thirty-five and still jumping
        off garage roofs as you did at five,

down-shattering your foot bones
and hobbling

for hours pretending your shoes
        don't hurt

as if to prove the body has its reasons
        which the brain

can stand–these manic highs of yours,
        these madman wings

that inevitably melt down their wax
        to solitude,

the ocean you so blithely flew as a teenager
        a weedy millpond

and the great sun
        a star so far gone

no one can touch it
with the most sensitive telescope.

Who can reach you—and what
        does the oracle say?

Years we have been moving apart
        and you never held

flights of conversation worth preserving-
        feather-soothing, louse-plucking

gnat-clouding-and the self?
 one more two-winged construct,

what's the point?
Don't you know I know

my briefest hug offends you.
You want me far away,

I want you to take
your medications

so that you can be a little more kin
and kind and I can say

I've been there, my child, I am there
now in that self-concerned pond

that flows nowhere, I too tried to fly
in my own grave

way and I still love you, child,
as I loved you as a child,

floating or falling,
        whatever flying means.

MARLENE MAE WARNS OF TRAVEL TO HER FORMER MARRIAGE

It seemed too good to be true,
a man who would come home from work
and gobble Gong Bao Chicken out of the box,

but after a month of schlepping from Sushi to Thai,
she learned there were restrictions:
just how much she could spend on cappuccinos

before mucking up the GNP. Always rumbles—
snow bursts, mud fits, tender tantrums, hissicanes.
Shopping malls, he warned,

were subject to conniption, earthquake.
Bushfires broke out every morning at 5 am
before she was entirely awake.

Stay out of grocery stores, he snarled one Tuesday,
flare-ups and meltdowns predicted.
Steer clear of Central Park,

those coyotes are easily mistaken for rabid dogs,
and no more nude swimming in the aboveground
        pool,
yes, there's a fence, but it's barbing local agitation,

haven't you noticed the drones buzzing overhead?
Soon the skirts he had chosen were too short
and the hair he had demanded too long.

He began to fine her for the way she squeezed
        toothpaste,
hand-jobs on the tube being subject to arrest.
If she didn't want to do things

as her good Lord and Master had ordained,
it was time to move to Singapore
where women are thonged for such things.

MARLENE MAE TALKS ABOUT DENIAL

When Daddy began his long forget,
stashing his checkbook in the potato bin,

Mother tried to teach him new things,
how to dry dishes and shatter them away

while my sister Alice Ann, our tried and crude
        believer,
maintained we could rebuild Pop's mind,

let the flood of forgetfulness become a drop in the
        shove-it,
shrink the mountain back to a molehill.

If he just played games, she said–
hearts, dominos, spin-the-bottle, pinochle, poker,
        chess–

he'd remember more and suffer less,
her old belief that self-help was as easy as whelping

which, birthing that ten-pound monstrosity of hers,
she should have known, was not.

Me, I knew all along, whatever Alice Ann said
about my hell-bound loss of hope and lack of faith,

our father's last tactic, repressing everything,
is what would save us,

who in their right mind
can bear what we have done?

MARLENE MAE'S MOTHER TURNS SEVENTY-SIX AND HER PHYSICIAN ASKS IF SHE IS STILL SEXUALLY ACTIVE

In bed they reach for each other and draw back.
She knows he can't or almost can't, he knows she
    won't
or will reluctantly. Afraid. She doesn't want him
to fail. Or feel he has failed. She wants to tell him
you can't fail me, not this corrugated body. *Never
let me go.* They talk medications, but she doesn't
    want
pulmonary distress, cardiac arrest, what if he died *in
    medias res.*
She'd have to wash herself and dress him before
    calling
911. How could she get his pants back on with her
    arthritic
thumbs. *Love me tender. Love me slow.*
How sore she used to get, but still sex was more
tic than *earthquake*. Sometimes she had wanted to
    ask
her friends if their sex was *tsunami*, but old
as she was, she was still shy, one of those timid
    bodies
who just didn't get it, the way she never got dirty
    jokes
in high school. What was she dreaming about then
when everyone else was thinking *love me tender,*
worrying about the Latin quiz, *amo, amas, amat.*
She certainly wasn't listening to the radio,
WHOT, Youngstown, Ohio, the hot spot on your
    dial.
No, safer conjugations: *amamus, amatis, amant.*
Amabamus, love, past imperfect, that made sense,
all that static hurt her ears and she fled to another
    room—
let her sister croon, *never let me go.*

I guess you could call it that, she says, but more *still* than *active*.

MARLENE MAE PAINTS HER MOTHER'S NAILS

Went to the mortuary the day before the viewing.
Just me and my emery boards in that cool room
and Momma covered with a sheet.

Mortician said his manicurist would do it,
but I remembered Aunt Lavinia,
pearl polish smeared on her cuticles.

Said the feet were going to be covered up
by the satin quilt, but Momma believed
you can tell a lady by her feet.

I painted her toes summer indigo
and glued on rhinestones. Stars, Momma,
you can walk on stars forever.

Then the hands, her little hands.
I wish I could have done the mouth.
Then it wouldn't have looked so strange.

GRANDMOTHER

Chalk becomes dust faster than flesh, said my grandmother,
dusting up her days school-marming children. Eventually,
she suffered one of her own, my father. One was
    enough.
No chalk to cheese for her. A second wife, she didn't
    want
to chalk up a second if it meant squeezing that
    double-
drunk into her double bed. Who knows where he
    slept
or what excuses she dusted off with her cheese-cloth
to displease him, she couldn't talk about that, not
    even hint
she had made a mistake marrying. Maybe
her glasses made him as good as it got, and she did
    get
my father who according to my grandmother was too
    good
for my mother and her fifth-grade *eddication.* So
    here's
Grandmother's picture from the one-room days
with her brothers and sisters. She's the one standing
as stiff as a pencil. Never many smiles
in that woman, but not yet wishing herself back
in the classroom, dusting that dirty farmer off her
    skin,
and he long gone before we came, my sister and I.
By then she couldn't dust him off for us, hanging as
    he was,
high up in the back of the barn, a man who had no
    words
or chalk to draw this woman who had a little
    education
back to him, just that one egg between them
which had been hers from the beginning, my father
whom she wanted to become a preacher, all her eggs

in that one basket. No place, said her old farmer.
No place for him.

THE TRUE BELIEVER WORKS IN THE VINEYARD

She wanted to be a good mother, raise good grub for healthy children, plant a goodly garden, one so decent no serpent, stink bug, slug dare invade, a patch unlike her childhood lot, that scrabble of bruised apples and tinned sardines, and for a June it seemed the tiny snaps and strings, fillets and romanos, would grow into perfect beans, wholesome fare for her boy, her girl.

But then the bean bugs came, first as clusters of translucent orange eggs, almost beautiful aliens, jewel-like, hundreds on the leafy underside, and then the little gems ballooned into spineless larvae, kidney-shaped, foreign, hairy and yellow, and she began to fight the good fight which her organic evangelists preached, one with blameless weapons, non-toxic pesticides whipped up in the same blender she used for her children's smoothies: a pepper soap froth of jalapeños, garlic, cloves, crushed egg shells, sure death to those soft-bellied fiends.

And as the good book recommended, she sprayed and sprayed every time it rained. We cannot say that she was not faithful.

But the little creeps multiplied like plague, and soon she had to kill with her bare fingers, squeeze them to death, drown them in her morning coffee and afternoon tea, teach her children to become fearless soldiers, do likewise, she said, live steadfast and unflinching, virtuous without poisoning the earth.

Yet the battle was not to the brave. Those bastards turned into polka-dotted beetles, armies of yellow helmets, too many to squeeze the living pus from. When at last the good fight was done, the bean leaves which had been luxurious and green had become brittle nets and the beans shriveled sticks in soil, starved fingers, pitted and sick, unfit for any of us to eat.

WOMAN FINDS HER FACE

when she unfolds the tablecloth
and then the stains of her bones, scapula,
radius, pelvis, and she realizes
she has been thinking about sorrow again.
How she doubles it around herself,
belly and back. What she can't change,
punctures circling forehead and scalp.
It's cold outside, ice sheets the gorge
down by the river, 30-degree drop
into hardness, her swollen face,
the telltale wounds of a Roman scourge,
the heart swells and loses elasticity.
Whom can she forgive? The boy who left
her daughter for Aspasia? The pedophile
who was her brother-in-law?
Or is it the old woman who demands
another invitation to dinner?
Everyone's hanging around the skull
like a Renaissance painting. No reciprocity.
Tit for tat. If she has the shroud,
what need crucifixion? Today you will dine with me
in paradise. Suppose someone
tested the image and said it goes back
to the beginning. No lie.
If ice didn't swell as it melted,
no one would be here. True too.
Her daughter said there are some things
we can't forgive—and others, what say the priests?
Something dirties the linen?

THE WIDOW'S SELF-PORTRAIT WITH QUICKSAND

In that dream we were walking
and then sinking–

scenario as trite as our hearts
but surprising to us

who thought ourselves immune
to gimmick,

didn't it just happen to others
in 60's flicks?

You dropped my hand
to save yourself

and I watched you sink
and then myself

as if we were two separate
stones.

SHELF-PORTRAIT

She put her body on the sill
with the dead possum curled
around its little heart,
its little paws. When
is she going to use it again?

Her pelvis
which framed the sky,
twilight twinning sun, dusk
and dawn, day moving
through her into dust,
it's been so long
since she shellacked her cranium
for an evening at the Moulin Rouge,
the delicate varnish, everyone
dressed in red.

Yes, you may touch her breasts,
take each down, hold one
in one hand, one in the other,
remember the feel
of small balloons in your palms
at the beginning of a water fight,
the heft of each soft globe.
Oh touch them, use them
for something . . . anything.

Author's Bio

Lois Marie Harrod's 16th and most recent collection *Nightmares of the Minor Poet* appeared in June 2016 from Five Oaks. *And She Took the Heart* (Casa de Cinco Hermanas) appeared in January 2016, *Fragments from the Biography of Nemesis* (Cherry Grove Press) and the chapbook *How Marlene Mae Longs for Truth* (Dancing Girl Press) appeared in 2013. *The Only Is* won the 2012 Tennessee Chapbook Contest (Poems & Plays), and *Brief Term*, a collection of poems about high school teachers and teaching was published by Black Buzzard Press, 2011. *Cosmogony* won the 2010 Hazel Lipa Chapbook (Iowa State). Dodge poet and 3-time recipient of a New Jersey Council on the Arts fellowship, she is widely published in literary journals and online ezines from *American Poetry Review* to *Zone 3*. Since 2006 she has taught creative writing at The College of New Jersey, literature courses at the Evergreen Forum in Princeton and has conducted writing workshops and poet-in-the classroom residencies.

Light's Music

by

Charlotte Mandel

*Remembering Manny
and for our children
grandchildren
and great-grandchildren*

Table of Contents

Acknowledgments	70
Stillness of Three a.m.	71
After Illness	72
Sunwarmed by the Pond	73
A Sequence for Ravi	75
To a Great-Grandchild Newborn	
One Year Old	
Couplets for a Two Year Old	
Fanfare for a Three Year Old	
Quatrains for a Four Year Old	
Beach Comber	80
Day's Birth	81
Small Child on a Beach	82
Light's Music	83
My Only First Cousin	84
Shofar	85
Passover	86
Kneading the Dough for Challah	87
Sufganiyot for Hannukah	88
A Pilgrim Returns for Succoth	89
Pathways	90
In a University Library	91
Housewarming Gifts	92
From a Grandmother	93
Mozart on a Winter Afternoon	94
Biography	95

Acknowledgments

Grateful acknowledgement is made to editors of the publications in which the following poems have appeared, sometimes in slightly different form.

Literature Today: "Couplets for a Two Year Old"
The Book of Donuts, Terrapin Press 2017: "Sufganiyot for Hannukah"
Poetry Parade 2018, Your Daily Poem: "Light's Music"
Your Daily Poem: "Mozart on a Winter Afternoon"
To Be the Daylight (Kelsay Books 2017); rpt. *arc-24*: "Shofar"

STILLNESS OF THREE A.M.

There are those who seek
a kind of breath
of light that
sees   hears

as a way to God

and to me?
I want to tear away the iconography
that enamels our thoughts
to images

shellacked   immovable
black lead outlines filled in with
mosaic
lessons of stained glass windows
so that dayight

illuminates the pre-set
justifies the pre-conceived
and yet
what is it that

can burden with love
as the abused child
craves
love the only way it knows?

There is a prayer
written in invisible ink
script that comes forth

in light
 bursting from underwater
when ocean quiets
during furthest ebb

AFTER ILLNESS
Lake Como, Italy

It is useful to die a little now and then.

The clarity of such a day

red sky darkening daylight in the valley
clouds like distant mountains.

There is an everlastingness that we cannot harm.
Recovery from illness
promises world won't end.

Overhanging branches tease the lake
with their reflections underwater.

I wish to dissolve
in quietly ominous water,
the path of sunset's shimmer
rising to rose-red smoke of the future
pressured by moment
becoming past.

Destiny is motion.
To foretell the flow
I must hold myself still.

SUNWARMED BY THE POND

Green the woods
Green the grassy banks
reflected in rippling water
Sunwarmed breeze
Flowering trees

Languages in the air - goldfinch trill -
cardinal whistle - crow's harsh caw

Thrum of a small plane overhead
out of nearby Totowa airport
Plane owners park their machines there
The Kennedy son, his wife and her sister flew in rainstorm
to death from there

How many do I outlive by now?

Where I live a table displays photos
captioned "in loving memory"
Today my glance afforded a sense of relief -
all clear on the table - death's taking a holiday
I recall the movie with "Death" as a character
played by a handsome star - and young heroine
in love with him
At the end he appears in black hooded cloak
"Now you see me as I really am." "But that is how
I've always seen you," she says

How shall I see "Death" when he/she/it
approaches to embrace
mind and body?
As a figure?
As a mist? Vision blur?
Voice - echo - spoken - sung?
As when falling asleep
unaware of moment of transition?
Loved faces surrounding?

Beloved lost husband
my life ever entwined with yours -
single root branching into
you
and me
and genealogies to come

A SEQUENCE FOR RAVI

To a Great-Grandchild Newborn

So now you've crossed the threshold,
entered our sphere of breath and sighs.
Welcome, new tenant, your soft limbs
safe in gravity's reliable embrace.
This is "world"—created of elements

set free by a wondrous explosion.
Little one, you've crowned
your intimate pulsing journey,
attained haven of young parents
joyfully amazed by downy fontanel,
birth-blue eyes awake/asleep,
rosy mouth's eagerness to suck.

Count others who adore you—
four grandparents and two
great-grandmothers. A universe
of cradling arms. Soon
you'll be able to see, tell us
one from another. And we will praise
your wondrous changes to come.

One Year Old

You came to us twelve months ago,
have now tested our varieties
of sun-warmth, brisk breezes,
icy winds, tree blossom fragrances.

What does not change
are the safe strong arms
of those who hold you,
the smiles of delight
on faces as you reach
push   kick   giggle   taste
and soothing voices
when you cry.

Fledgling in the nest
learning to sing
day by day
words and music
you compose
sure of your place in the world.

Grateful, we accept your gift.

Turning Two

You're at an age of doubled charm, boisterous,
wiser than we know, the world's your oyster—

quick fingers pry, open, discover pearls
of fun as you slide, climb, leap, spin, twirl

in time to a song in your toy smart phone,
sneeze in Daddy's face, blink at Mommy's tone

of voice—and answer "No!" Oh, what positive
power of self such a negative can give!

Grownups read you stories and you can talk
in turn with stories—like the time you walked

"in a bed. . .got a bump"—but after bruise,
got kisses. Your laugh melts away the blues.

Running into our arms you win the race
transforming our world to merry-go-round space.

Fanfare for a Three Year Old

What game shall you play today? So aware,
debonair, choosing a t-shirt to wear.
Your computer photos gift me with rare

joy of blessed thankfulness, to share
that confident pride with which you dare
to run to slide to swoop anywhere

the soccer ball may roll. Devil-may-care
you run round the bases with time to spare
and catch the world at home plate. You're an heir

to city, river, sea and thoroughfare.
We send you sunshine in our every prayer
for the fun that life is, your dimpled flair

to smile, love, embrace. Lifted in mid-air
you know you're safe. *Mere, pere, grandpere, grandmere*—
Bubbe, Paca, Maga, Awja, G.G.'s who stare

at Skype screens and sing, "Beyond compare!"
May our planet join hands with you in a square
dance, surrounded by stars. Let candles flare—

one   two   three   count   blow   and trumpets blare!

Quatrains for a Four Year Old

Now you sleep in a big-boy bed,
dance with Amazing Arlington Tots
colorful in costumes gold and red,
play with tiles and connect the dots.

You've moved into Daddy's office space,
discovered sports as part of a team
in yellow vests running a soccer race,
then licking melt-in-your-mouth ice cream.

You can help to put your toys away,
go swimming with cousins and friends,
trace initial R at school today,
show proudly at home when school day ends.

You hug the persons loved the most
rewarding those who love you with joy,
giving us reason to happily boast
of a brilliant, self-confident, blessed little boy.

BEACH COMBER

The sound of breaking waves
reverberates
in my brain.

Foot soles recall
sand's soothing friction
on edges of foam
heels racing
cold surf's
rush to bury the dunes.

Fingers grainy with sand
scoop up sun-baked gifts of past tides,
layer white clam shells
one upon the next larger
and seek unbroken
lush purple spirals of moon snail.

But the rise and fall of waves
brings other
unwanted gifts—ocean currents swirl
bottle relics of our thirst for flavored drinks
plastic bags afloat like dead jellyfish

into a mass mid-ocean
marine debris
locked against marine lives.

I wash the sand from shells
losing salt redolence
the clue to their births and passings in sea

and in me
the wash of waves breaking on shore
sounds on and on.

DAY'S BIRTH

Rainwater breaks through
and stills

No wind

Gray skim overhead
begins to fray

Light
bears down

Clouds exhale and part

Shadows come forth

SMALL CHILD ON A BEACH

Your arms shatter the dunes
in one breast stroke,
remorseless as bulldozers
shearing the plain.

Your fist gouges a canyon
displacing a cliff of earth.
You clap the new mountain into dominance
then cleave a valley through its peak.

Your pail of water ordains a lake
as source of a river.
Current glides to your conducting
until you dam its flow.

Omnipotent lordling
recapitulating Genesis
you must grow taller soon
and lose supremacy.

LIGHT'S MUSIC
To Dina, as you expect your second child

sun rising on a mountain peak's
snow covered rock
rays firing into a roseate sky
dawn's afterglow

full moon's maternal/paternal face
appearing pale at twilight until

brilliant lamp haloed in midnight blue
beams a road of rippling sparkle
onto calm ocean
susurrus of quiet foam on sand

in a moonless sky
the stars take over
constellations
guiding travelers
uncounted millenia
since our galaxy's birth

and within you shines
warm invisible glow
of new life

MY ONLY FIRST COUSIN
in memoriam R. G.

Israel to me is Rochel, my only
cousin from the *shtetl* birthplace
of my mother, also Rochel. My mother's
brother's daughter, the only
daughter or sister or father or brother or
grandfather or aunt, grandmother, or
infant—how many degrees of immediate
family closeness to name, only
known in grainy darkening photographs—

except you, from the camps to Cyprus
island where you met a sweet husband, only
to lose him too soon, raising
two daughters and a son. And discovered
me, an American cousin. Saturday mornings,
blessed Yiddish enabled our voices to sing
across continental spaces. Only

once you visited my home, only
once I celebrated Passover at your home,
where the youngest grandchild easily
asked four questions in his native Hebrew.
And that night was truly
different from all other nights.

SHOFAR

Lay your ear to an austere mound
of hard-packed sands: clustered sounds

preserve syllables of Aramaic
counterpoint with near-lost Judaic,

Phoenician, Egyptian, Babylonian,
enriched by diaspora's loans

to birth of twenty-first century
Hebrew: ancient psalms rendered

for newsprint, emails, election
ballots, parliamentary sections,

supermarkets, medical corps,
days of a calendar luni-solar.

Tightened lips on the polished horn
sound to the year at sunset: *Turn*

away from guilts, remorse and strife,
taste honeyed fruits of blessed life.

Calling the children of Abraham,
Saved, as Isaac, by horn of a ram.

PASSOVER

The wine we drink
is made from grapes
planted in a vineyard
five thousand years ago.

The matzo we bless and break
is baked from flour harvested
as stalks of wheat, cut
by hand with sickle blades,
winnowed, threshed and flailed,
five thousand years ago.

The lamb, the bitter herbs, all
the ritual foods on our plates,
we tasted and ate
five thousand years ago.

Each crumb, morsel, drop we take,
is a memory.
We are there
as we are here
alive today
because of
five thousand years ago.

KNEADING THE DOUGH FOR CHALLAH

My mother would squeeze
and roll
clumps of flour-dusted dough

left hand forward
right hand back.

My small hands would try
and try to follow her
left hand forward
right hand back

dispirited
by clumsy lack of rhythm.

Watching her twenty years later
in eureka moment
realize
why of course!

she was working the dough
lefthanded

and my righthanded self
inefficient with the left
could never match.

She cut the dough in strips
rubbed between palms
formed into braid.

My consolation would be
the extra braided small challah

brushed with egg to shine
in the child-size loaf pan
baked for me alone.

SUFGANIYOT FOR HANNUKAH

Holiday foods unite spirit with body—
for Hannukah, sufganiyot—
round jelly doughnuts dusted
with powdered sugar. Fried in oil
the treat recalls ancient miracle—

how a sacred flame with but one day's pour of oil
shone radiant seven days more until
newly purified oil of olive,
fragrant with myrrh and cinnamon,
could be brought across desert.

On Israeli streets
kiosks spring up fast as dandelions.
Faces of children and their parents
jelly-streaked, lips sugar-layered.
Sparrows pouncing on crumbs.

So delicious to so many
that the Minister of Health
warns of overeating,
and even an Orthodox rabbi
writes in a daily paper, "no need
to fatten our children."

At sundown
parents kindle menorah candles.
Orange-gold flames reflect in children's eyes
as sufganiyot appear on their plates
eight successive days.

A PILGRIM RETURNS FOR SUCCOTH

I'm stranded on this shore,
sands blown from eroded pyramids.
Across a false sea
wavers Judea's landscape.
By what tree will I recognize my courtyard?

No boat sails this mirage.
Still, I have a canteen of fresh water.
The map draws a house made of twigs,
baskets of dried figs and almonds
tied to elbows of branches.

No salt in this wind, only the sharp
scents of grinding spices,
tang of citrus assure my return.
A full moon will light the harvest
of wandering days.

PATHWAYS
for Blanche

Your face had begun to unveil
the skull in wait.

In the full of our flesh, we treat bones
as hoists, a handy armature.

"I have a lot of stamina,"
you said, unafraid to boast.

"Be careful, touch wood, spit
three times."

"Not to worry—here, catch—"
you blew me a kiss.

Something of you, stationed
within me, flashes

arrows of light, signaling
pathways.

We are small animals
balancing on a rock promontory.

What rope, wire, radiowave
might connect us now

when I surround the hollow
of your memory

in my body
choked with life?

IN A UNIVERSITY LIBRARY

Do students know their beauty
as they stride
on polished black and white tiles?

They intersect at random
passing me as though I'm adrift
on a river raft

a youth sailing on such handsomeness
my armchair rocks in his wake.

Why does this parade
strike me with memory's cudgel?

> —when I saw my newborn's
> moist fluttering fingers
> helpless to brush a speck of dust
> from an eyelash
>
> that her every comfort
> depended on a stiff-armed adolescent
> chilled by sudden omnipotence—

Mother of grown children, let me cease
to seek forgiveness in a line of typed letters.

Each child has met me face to face
with force of inborn self-to-be.

Here on the border of fleeting
patterns of book-laden dance

listening to voices phrasing
contrapuntal mother tongues

my harbor awaits.

HOUSEWARMING GIFT

*Bread that this house may never know hunger
Salt that life may always have flavor*

Salt:
comes easy
to the tongue's curl

Millenial rains
cascade down
mountains
dissolving

into the sea's
white peaks

Minute glints in our cells
keep us alive

Bread:
teaches concept—
how act follows handful of seed

dig: sow: reap: grind: knead

Round ovens and square—
let guests come to share

Fire
heats and we eat

FROM A GRANDMOTHER
to Benjamin / to Avi
written when you were very little

to tell you
your faces are gold discs bubbling at the top of a spring-fed lake
your mouths a rich tease of sunfish dragonfly and laughter
sighting a child self who laughs in the ripples your eyes the wise
gaze of waterlilies opening to a gliding raft

your bodies rise to wonders of knowing hour by hour the pace
of your constant becoming I have loved you from the first notice
given me of your existence to this minute second instant and know
 this, know that I will love you through all your transformations

and my own
If there is existence in the particles I will set free then each speck
will signal strong and beneficent, a blink of my
clear and present wonder

MOZART ON A WINTER AFTERNOON

duo

Bows upon strings, violin and viola
sound notes light as gauze wings
of a dragonfly touching a stone
risen in the midst of a mountain brook
or whirling foam of rapids
loud as applause

quartet

Cello and another violin add
deepening river currents
flashes of silver scales
quick quivering fins

quintet

With clarinet the widening stream
flows past moss fringed with blue thyme
willow branches swaying to test
reflections in sun-and-shade dappled water
air echoing birds whistles and trills

audience

"Heaven," sighs a listener.
Cheers reverberate to stained glass windows

We exit bundled against wintry wet wind
with visions of waist-high sunflowers
sibilant violet surf rinsing white sands
a rare cloud or two sailing
faultless blue

Author's Bio

Charlotte Mandel has published eleven books of poetry, the most recent, *Alive and In Use: Poems in the Japanese Form of Haibun.* Previous titles include *To Be the Daylight; Through a Garden Gate*—poems responding to color photographs by Vincent Covello; *Life Work; Rock Vein Sky;* and two poem-novellas of feminist biblical revision—*The Life of Mary* and *The Marriages of Jacob.* Her awards include the New Jersey Poets Prize, two fellowships in poetry from New Jersey State Council on the Arts; Woman of Achievement (arts); and residencies at Yaddo, Millay, VCCA, and Villa Montalvo. She edited the Eileen W. Barnes Award Anthology, *Saturday's Women.* Critical essays include a series on the role of cinema in the life and work of H.D., articles on Muriel Rukeyser, May Sarton, Thomas McGrath, and others. Visit her at www.charlottemandel.com.

Critical Praise

Descendants of Eve is an engagement with the every-day practice of joy, of faith and faithfulness, rendered with precision and tenderness. Sachs examines the varieties of love—parental, romantic, spiritual, ecological, generation—through the lens of her own conception and practice of Judaism; or maybe she examines Judaism through the varieties of love. This book is a delight—never sentimental, but full of sentiment of the most thought-filled kind. —Marcela Sulak

Carly Sachs's poems are drawn from deep aquifers of love. They bring us sustenance. They buzz with a quiet electricity and pulse with a connection to the divine. "The body is a music," she writes in "Clarification." Her poems resonate with unseen threads of longing and weave a whole through the artistry and honesty of her language in the visible air. —David Hassler, Director, Wick Poetry Center at Kent State University

Rooted in the *moss and mushroom* of the female body, the poems in Lois Marie Harrod's chapbook, *Woman,* refreshingly skirt the merely celebratory. Harrod's natural music, sharp observations and sly wit bring a quirky authenticity to her tales of women often silenced, missing parts, or completely disassembled. With deeply resonant language and a robust measure of magical realism, Harrod's poems are inventive, bold, and fiercely poignant. —Catherine Doty, *Momentum*

Lois Marie Harrod's new collection, titled simply (but not so simply) *Woman,* crackles with brilliantly provocative imagery that follows the arc of the work and keeps the reader engaged. The poems command attention in an unexpected way; the reader is allowed to move only at the pace of a symbolic *Everywoman.* Harrod's Woman is the "Weaker vessel [even] Plato/could not shadow/or shut down" of her title poem, and Woman is the speaker in "Shelf-Portrait," the final poem which skillfully picks up the despair of a widow. Woman is Marlene Mae who gives the living a legacy by painting her dead mother's toenails celestial indigo. Harrod seems to say Woman, like Life, must go on. She reminds us that though Woman may lose her way, she will find herself again and put herself back together because no shelf or shadow is vast enough to contain her. After all, it is *her* "pelvis that frames the sky" and her pelvis that ushers in humanity, sustains it and prevents its extinction. Indeed, *Woman* is a blueprint for resilience.— Gretna Wilkinson, PhD. Founder, The Raven's Porch

I have loved Charlotte Mandel's work for a long, long time, and this new chapbook does not disappoint; rather, it's another chapter in her distinguished work. In *Light's Music*, Mandel sings of darkness, the losses that tally in these final decades, her own death yet to come, but also of light, a blessing for a new great-grandchild, poems of his first four years. This music runs through poems of family, poems of nature, poems of Jewish tradition and culture, all falling lightly from her pen. "A full moon will light the harvest / of wandering days." Mandel writes in "A Pilgrim Returns for Succoth," and these fine poems will light the path for poetry lovers everywhere. —Barbara Crooker, author of *The Book of Kells* (Cascade Books)

In *Light's Music*, Charlotte Mandel focuses on both beginnings and ends. In her grandchildren and great grandchildren, she celebrates new life and her legacy going forward, her Jewish heritage honored and preserved—all from a voice reconciling and making close getaways from the inevitable as she prepares for the day "shadows come forth" and she can "dissolve" and rise "to rose-red smoke." This chapbook is a strong distillation of precision in poetry and hope for us all. —Mary Frances Wagner, author *The Immigrants' New Camera*

More from BLP

Delphi Series Vol. 1

Anna Leahy
Karen L. George
Robert Perry Ivey

Delphi Series Vol. 2

Joy Ladin
Jennifer Litt
Tasha Cotter

Delphi Series Vol. 3

Aaron Bauer
Francine Rubin
Meghan Sterling

Delphi Series Vol. 4

Ting Gou
Claire Zoghb
Erin Redfern

Delphi Series Vol. 5 (fiction)

Diane Payne
Lana Spendl
Chella Courington

Delphi Series Vol. 6

Allison Blevins
Saul Hillel Benjamin
Cameron Morse

Delphi Series Vol. 7

Marjorie Power
Sally Zakariya
Martha McCollough

Delphi Series Vol. 8 (this issue)

Charlette Mandel
Carly Sachs
Lois Marie Harrod

Delphi Series Vol. 9 (forthcoming)

Susanna Lang
Jennifer Grant
Christina Lovin

Delphi Series Vol 10 (to be announced)

www.ingramcontent.com/pod-product-compliance
Lightning Source LLC
Chambersburg PA
CBHW051658040426
42446CB00009B/1202